KEEPING
TIME

KEEPING
TIME

Suzanne Cleary

Carnegie Mellon University Press
Pittsburgh 2002

ACKNOWLEDGMENTS

Grateful acknowledgment is made to the following publications in which some of
these poems originally appeared:

Atlanta Review: "On Learning of a Book by Arthur Debles Entitled *How to Distinguish
the Saints in Paintings By Their Costumes, Symbols, and Attributes*"
Beloit Poetry Journal: "The Docks of New York"
London Daily Telegraph: "Great Grandfather"
Georgia Review: "Study," "Yasmin"
Massachusetts Review: "Sewing in January"
New Letters: "This," "Though the Grass," "Thrift Shop"
Ohio Review: "Friday Meditation," "Girls' School," "Labyrinthitis,"
"Summary of 15 Years"
Poetry: "Girl in Mourning," "Listening to the Poem," "Stock Footage"
Poetry Northwest: "Acting," "All at Once," "Almost Away," "The Horse Latitudes,"
"Madame Beaumont"
Prairie Schooner: "Amaryllis," "Ivory Bracelets"
Southern Poetry Review: "Birdsall Street," "There is No Such Thing as Moonlight"
Southern Review: "There are People Who Cannot Cross Bridges Without Wanting
to Jump"
Third Coast: "Country"
U.S.: National Civics in a Mosaic Democracy: "Ivory Bracelets"

Certain of these poems won awards and/or appeared in anthologies:
"Great Grandfather" was a Second Prize winner in the Arvon International Poetry
Competition (1998). "This," "Though the Grass" and "Thrift Shop" won the New
Letters Literary Award in Poetry (1994). "Almost Away" won the Cecil Hemley
Memorial Award from the Poetry Society of America (1993). "There is No Such
Thing as Moonlight" won the Guy Owen Poetry Award (1992). "The Horse Latitudes"
won Second Prize in the Billee Murray Denny Poetry Competition (1992) and
appeared in *Imperiled Landscapes* (Rizzoli 1997). "On His Deathbed the Acrobat Tells
His Daughter to Buy Land" appeared in the *Sotheby's International Poetry Competition
Anthology*, 1982, Third Prize winner.

Book design by Emily Landes

The publication of this book is supported by a grant from the
Pennsylvania Council on the Arts.

Library of Congress Control Number: 2001089536
ISBN: 0-88748-363-1 Pbk.
Printed and bound in the United States of America

10 9 8 7 6 5 4 3 2 1

CONTENTS

For my parents,
where these poems began.

SUMMARY OF FIFTEEN YEARS
for M.H.

I will tell the best and the worst,
Paris 5 a.m., trucks from the countryside, men handing down
crates, women unpacking raspberries and pears,
my apartment in Queens, on the windowsill
a persimmon, flesh like sunset,
softening, growing sweet. I am in love
with loneliness, a man who lives far away.
He plays the harmonica and is afraid of thunder,
There is a black cotton dress, how, wearing it
I feel, for the first time, beautiful.
There is my first taste of plum wine,
my first serious lie. I scream, alone
in my car, I scream at the rain.
There is pain in my back
and x-rays pouring through my body
like rain through a screen door.
In Webster Groves, Missouri, a photograph
is taken: I wear a fur coat from the 40s
under a bank temperature sign, 104 degrees.
This is the year of trying too hard
followed by the year of not caring.
One night there is a lake, invisible in darkness,
not shining until I touch it.
There are eyes, green, dark brown, I step into
to never fully return. At some point I begin
to call strangers' children Honey.
There is someone I love, a hospital bed,
a green stain on the pillowcase.
A white dog runs out of the fog
like part of the fog, into my headlights.
I clean out my grandmother's house,
find my grandfather's skinny undershirts

threadbare, freshly washed.
Then there is someone whispering into my ear, again,
after I had forgotten the feel of that,
then there is only the memory of it,
for there is imagined memory now.
There are gifts: a silver pin I wear on my coat,
a barrette that falls from my hair,
a man kneeling beside me, saying,
I want you to always remember this morning,
and there is what he does next.
There is the loss of my mother's ring, there is seeing
the hair on my father's chest is white
and there is not knowing, finally,
what to call joy and what grief,
but wanting to tell it all in one breath
so I will be here, and you.

STOCK FOOTAGE

An avalanche, a flock of geese, fire,
a river rising into flood,
mostly stock footage is nature, stilled
and locked away in darkness,
waiting for its cue.
But if the script calls for the young pilot
to disappear at sea, there is a ten-second shot
of the round-nosed plane of my father's youth,
the plane threading through the clouds like it has found Heaven
while the camera backs away and the clouds fold
over the silver wings.
If the pilot must crash on land, there is another film.
This footage exists because each crash is the same
though we wish this were not true.
It is rewound, endlessly, ready at the next call for disaster.
The plane, the geese, the waters
wait, still, in the dark
though their true medium is time and light
and that place in the mind where we want to believe.
Seeing that plane I think of second grade,
classes crowded together in the school library
watching the television: a rocket rises into the sky
like a knife tearing silk.
I hear my father's voice, that day and others,
saying, "This is history, Suze. This is something to remember,"
and I see him, wearing the red and blue plaid bathrobe
he wore in those years.
In the realm of stock footage is there anyone
who can stand for him? Yes.
Also there are lovers, nude, embracing on the beach.
Seen from great distance, we can mistake them for ourselves.
There is a one-mile stretch of road lined with palm trees
that, spliced into a circle, will serve as the route
for a hundred California car trips,

because it is the mind that sees,
embellishes. Because time and light
and that place in the mind where we want to believe
carry us, propel us
through that space filled by stock footage,
through that time when the flock of geese inside our shoulders
suddenly rises, calling,
or when the flood water inside our chest, flashes
white and pounding, furiously
braiding itself into the air.

THERE ARE PEOPLE WHO CANNOT CROSS BRIDGES
WITHOUT WANTING TO JUMP

I've read of them, the desire in their soles,
their arms swaying like willow beside the banks.
I am not one of them. I stare at the river and think of love.
I stare at the muddy water gone clear toward the center, the deepest
part,
this clear water gone opaque with doubling back, triangular waves
beaded with white, self-contained light.
I grasp the rail. Do the jumpers fear what they desire?

When I say "of love" I mean for my hometown, with its two rivers,
the iron bridge the shoe workers crossed on foot
to get to the factory, my two grandmothers among them.
I mean love for my grandmothers, young, glad for the work,
love for the diner that overlooks the Chenango,
the dam you can see from the back booths, the rapids
a white tube of water like a fluorescent bulb.
I mean love for the place where the Chenango and the Susquehanna
converge, so you don't know what to call that spot.
And I mean hatred for the terrible factory
where my grandmothers bowed their smooth faces
and scarred their graceful hands.
I mean hatred for the power of that dam
to draw children, who believe their friends are immortal.

In the distance the water's surface looks smooth
and the river banks seem to touch, as if the eye were determined
to, finally, make everything meet.
Do the jumpers close their eyes, before?

I think maybe those people who would jump from bridges
are like the doe licking salt from the road
when the car's headlight appears and that light
is the same light inside the doe's eye, and so she leaps
to bring the lights together, as the waves do,
as lovers do, in their lapping.

BIRDSALL STREET

In 1944 you could buy a metal lawn chair from Montgomery Ward
for $2.50, red, green or yellow.
My grandparents bought two, banana-colored, set them beside
the tomato garden, and through the summer of '44
sat in their new chairs in the dark yard
smoking cigarettes as the fireflies came out,
their orange lights sharp and brief.

It was a summer of grieving for my grandmother's youngest brother,
lost in the Pacific, grieving as they mowed the lawn
and trimmed the hedges, grieving as they set window screens
against the porch steps and hosed them
until the silver mesh glistened like a lake glistens
with whatever light there is, whatever wind.
My grandparents worked until the light was gone
then sat in their chairs in the dark yard.

Twenty years later I sat in those chairs and I tell you
they were like brand new. Each evening my grandmother wiped them
and my grandfather carried them, one in each hand,
into the garage for the night.
Twenty years after that, I see one of these chairs,
the bottle-green, rusted and bent in front of an antique shop,
a page from the Montgomery Ward catalog taped to its arm.
How do I recognize it? It is an awkward chair,
cross between ice tongs and a soap dish.
I touch the seat and remember burning my legs
on the sun-heated metal, and recall that as the sun went down
my grandparents' chairs grew nail-cold.
It is a heavy chair, yet brittle.

When I kneel beside it, again I am watching
my grandmother wipe down the chairs.
She uses one of my grandfather's old undershirts
and brisk, circular motions on the back and seat.
She kneels to wipe the legs. The grass is dark and wet.
I am a darker shadow on the shadowed lawn, watching.
She is telling me that things must be cared for.
Without a word she tells me. It is two years
before her final grieving, which would last twenty more.
My grandfather touches her shoulder, takes her hand.
The chairs are shining, buttery even in darkness.
I am young enough to think they will be there forever,
the chairs, my grandparents, the shining.

ALL AT ONCE

I thought, Am I dead?
my mother says, in the tone you would say,
Is it raining? Are we out of milk?
She is telling me how my father came out of the restroom
to find her slumped over the table
and the waitress, who happened to also be a nurse,
holding her wrist, saying, "I can't find her pulse."
When my mother says this she's not going for humor
though humor is there, and more surely
than when she tells jokes, which she cannot do
because— I've puzzled over this— the jokes are real for her,
their silly, buffoonish people are real for her.
When she tells the one about the anonymous twin bell ringers
who pass through town one after the other
and both meet untimely deaths, and, finally,
she says, "I don't know
but he's a dead ringer for that other guy,"
you don't feel like laughing,
and today, telling this story, she's going for accuracy.
She could hear the voices of the nurse-waitress and my father,
could hear sounds from the kitchen, water and plates,
but everything was black, it was like the time
she fainted at the 1964 World's Fair.
Afterwards my sister and father and I
were taken to a small room with her,
all of us given glasses of water.
Then we were led to the front of the line,
given the next turn on the Goodyear Ferris wheel.
It was like the World's Fair, she has said,
and I have seen that even at such times,
the wife collapsed on the tablecloth,
the husband helpless at her side,
it's like something else.
Nothing is singular, simple.
While my mother is telling me about collapsing in a restaurant

I am thinking of the dresses my sister and I wore,
white piquees, mine with lavender flowers,
hers with turquoise. I am remembering
that I helped choose the fabric,
if you ran your fingers lightly across it
they tickled and felt numb.
I suppose that when my mother is slumped over her dinner plate
and the nurse-waitress lifts her hand
she doesn't feel her hand rising,
she feels nothing, and I think
maybe that's what she felt when I was a child—
four kids, no car, a husband working two jobs
to pay for the house near the shoe factory.
I remember her at my age, standing on the back porch
with a cloth in her hand, the white banister sparkling
with soot fallen during the night
as if the night itself had broken apart
in flakes, and settled, blackness and starlight together.
She wipes down the webbed lawnchairs,
turning the cloth in her hand, folding it,
this morning she has woken before
her children, her husband.
I have come to the back door in my pajamas.
I remember how she looked at me.
It wasn't love exactly, but love inexactly,
imperfect as it always is.
My presence had broken something
and I knew this because I was still
partly her, and so the breaking was inside of us both.
My mother tells me that it must have been the flu,
everyone's had the flu, and later that evening
she felt good enough to hose down the window screens.
It's spring already. "Here, too," I say.

For the past five minutes I have been staring
out the window. In the past 24 hours
the maple has blossomed, impossibly green.
How do the buds know to bud all at once,
I've wondered. How does the tree know
exactly what to do?

GREAT GRANDFATHER

Your son, nine, works
in the barber shop, sweeping hair from the floor,

stirring lather in small heavy bowls.
You are proud of this. Next year

he will leave school, and begin
being paid for his work.

You save to buy him the tools
of his trade: metal combs,

scissors (one long and one short),
razor with a first set of blades.

It is a good thing to work indoors
and not in the fields.

It is a good thing to work in daylight
and not in the mines.

In your house, by the front door
hangs a shaving mirror,

its silver worn half away,
but in the barber shop

your son polishes a mirror
so perfect it is invisible.

In it, your son can see himself
from head to knees.

The white starched apron covers him
to the tops of his shoes,

your firstborn, the one
who always climbed from his bed.

You had to tie the hem of his nightgown
to the bed post, so he would not wander.

No fear of the dark, your son crawled
through the night hallway,

miner's son, and only you would hear him,
his hand-pats on the floor

like water dripping through a fault.

ON LEARNING OF A BOOK BY ARTHUR DEBLES ENTITLED
HOW TO DISTINGUISH THE SAINTS IN PAINTINGS
BY THEIR COSTUMES, SYMBOLS, AND ATTRIBUTES

Monsieur DeBles, sometimes I miss the saints—
St. Elizabeth with her lapful of roses,
St. Veronica carrying the cloth
with which she wiped the face of Jesus,
St. Lucy, with the terrible wound
at her throat, streaming rays of light—

not that I prayed to them
or believed they prayed for me,
but that I believed so deeply
in their stories, their beauty,
that I took them for granted,

so that upon learning of your book
I marvel at your homage,
your life spent looking for saints,
white gloves folded in your back pocket,
magnifying glass dangling beneath your shirt.

From your prose I surmise
you were a modest man, content
to identify what others had wrought,
the entry for St. Isidore the Ploughman
exemplary: "Labourer's dress. Spade.

Angel ploughing in background."
You describe "the faithful," who are not saints
but are often in their company.
You display a special fondness for the nameless
shepherd in a grey robe, "the colour of humility,"

listening to John the Baptist.
You note the shepherd's hem is frayed on one side.

One of his legs must be shorter.
When he walks he sways
as Jesus must have, walking on water.

You address the animals who accompany the saints,
Benedict, for example, signaled
by a raven with a loaf of bread in his beak.
Methodical without losing your sense of wonder,
you note "lion with wings," "lion without wings."

Sometimes the saint is a child.
Sometimes the saint is a sinner, lost
in a crowd, or in thought,
an unlikely target for divine grace.
You study the saint at all ages, your book like Heaven

in that "in Heaven there is no time."
You write, "Paintings of Heaven contain anachronisms
because in Heaven all times exist at once,"
lest viewers argue inaccuracy
where there can be no inaccuracy.

In Heaven, approximation is beautiful.
It is only on earth we believe in perfection.
Last week, Monsieur DeBles, in an antique shop,
I found a Mexican santo
and stroked its uneven wings

and the dove it cradled, carved
from the same piece of wood as the saint.
I want to love what is of the earth.
As I love the grandmothers who say the rosary,
prayers like small seeds ground between teeth.

Monsieur DeBles, Heaven and earth at once.
Do we find this only in work?

AMARYLLIS

for Brian O'Connell

The day he dies a stranger buys a cut flower
and settles into painting the beautiful passages
from deep pink to vanilla, the cream
of pure white bathed with indirect light.
Her strokes are quick, knowing she cannot keep pace
                                        with the amaryllis.
See how the petals strain from the green knob and arch
outwards, as if to touch as much space as possible?
See how the thick stem pulls downwards and at the water's surface
seems to swell and bend, too large for the vase?
We live by illusions.
She notices she has forgotten the yellow tips of the pistil
and dots them in, floating,
where the flower casts shadow on itself, where the shadow-flower
                                                    grows
and connects with the air the living breathe.
Now she touches the next blossom. Her strokes loosen.
There is no need for the lines to connect. She could be
painting water, which has arranged itself into the shapes
of a flower, on its way to the sea.

GIRL IN MOURNING

after Paul Klee

The burnt end of a stick scratches
one line in the dirt: forehead, nose,
lips pressed together.
It is a thick line, this margin
between her face and what has become sky.
The line is charcoal on peach earth.
It is a fragile medium.
Wind can enter the ash, and lift it,
lift this sorrow out of the personal.

ALMOST AWAY

after "Old Gold Over White" by Mark Rothko

Two squares floating
on a peach-colored ground,
one

the gold of a copper clothes-kettle,
the other
the green-white of sweetpeas,

color without object
becomes color as object,
planes become places:

a frost-covered lawn,
one square of the plaid blanket
a man keeps in his car trunk.

There must be a way to live
without being in the world,
without being myself-in-the-world.

All the edges are hazy,
seem to tremble,
the small movements

of emphasis, erasure.
Inside, mottled, gauze-like,
the brushstrokes are visible,

the hand, one could say,
present,
its thinking

present, product.
It is not enough
to be productive

but to understand you have been
so. I am looking
for the place of importance,

the plane
of standing barefoot in wet grass,
breath taken

almost away
with the coolness.
There must be a way

to be free of the body,
free of scale,
the world of the painting entirely

spirit, though texture
implies touch,
implicates

the desire to touch.
There must be a way
to be free of the self

free of seeing oneself
in everything,
where it does not belong.

GLORY

My husband and his first wife once sang Handel's *Messiah*
at Carnegie Hall, with 800 others who also had read
the ad for the sing-along, and this is why I know
the word *glory* is not sung by the chorus,
although that is what we hear.
In fact, the choir sings *glaw-dee, glaw-dee*
while it seems that *glory* unfurls there, like glory itself.
My husband sings for me. My husband tells me they practiced
for an hour, led by a short man with glasses,
a man who made them sing *glory* twice, so they could hear it
fold back upon itself, swallow itself
in so many mouths, in the grand hall.
Then he taught them *glaw-dee,* a distortion that creates the right
effect, like Michelangelo distorting the arms of both God and Adam
so their fingertips can touch.
My husband and his first wife and 800 others performed
at 5 o'clock, the Saturday before Christmas,
for a small audience of their own heavy coats,
for a few ushers arrived early, leaning on lobby doors.
But mostly they sang for themselves,
for it is a joy to feel song made of the body's hollows.
I do not know if their marriage, this day, was still good
or whether it seemed again good
as they sang. I prefer to think of the choral conductor,
who sang with them. He sang all the parts, for love
not glory, or what seemed to be
glory to those who wandered in
and stood at the back of the hall, and listened.

ADAM AND EVE FROM PERU

The artist who has fashioned Adam and Eve from paper mache
makes them stand facing each other, but far enough apart
they must step forward to touch.
Adam's right arm is extended toward Eve, and Eve's
right arm is extended across her chest toward Adam.
Either of them would be able to hold
one of the tree's orange-red apples
in their well-formed hands.
Adam's hair covers his ears and Eve's hair covers her breasts.
Their hair is so black it looks blue, it looks wet.
Maybe there was a pond in the Garden of Eden
that has since been forgotten.
Maybe Adam and Eve have been swimming, and this accounts
for the heaviness in their bodies, the heaviness of earth after water.
Adam and Eve have already eaten from the Tree of Knowledge
for their genitals are covered with the leaves of paradise.
After the fall it is still paradise.
The tree is still beautiful, shining
as if with sunlight and rain at once,
its crescent leaves a green found only in Peru.
For the artist the world is paradise.
For Adam and Eve it is still paradise even according to Milton,
who changes their voices after they eat
so they speak familiarly. The range of their expression
opens. It includes anger, and silence, mercy.
They have become human, though they will not be rewarded
for completing God's work. They no longer belong
here, where the angel will find them, and lead them out,
here, this shining place they will not remember
except for a tart juice on the tongue
that could be the pond, the apple, each other.

ACTING

I most remember the class where we lie
on our backs, on the cold floor, eyes closed, listening
to a story set in tall grasses, a land of flash floods.
Ten babies slept in a wagon as a stream risen from nothing
trampled like white horses toward them.
We heard the horses, pulling their terrible silence.
Then he asked us to open our eyes. Our teacher
took from his pocket an orange square, dropped it:
this had wrapped one of the babies.
This was found after the water receded.

I remember the woman with red hair
kneeling before the scarf, afraid to touch it,
our teacher telling her she could stop
by saying, *OK, Good.*
I remember the boy named Michael, who
once told me he loved me. Michael
approached with tiny steps, heel to toe,
as if he were measuring land,
and, all at once, he fell
on the scarf. It could have been funny,
loud, clumsy. Another context, another moment,
it would have been ridiculous.
Head down, he held the scarf to his eyes.

My turn, I didn't move. I stared
at the orange scarf, but not as long
as I'd have liked to, for this was a class
and there were others in line for their grief.
I touched it, lightly, with one hand,
folded it into a square, a smaller square, smaller.

What is lived in a life?
Our teacher making up that story
as he watched us lie on the dusty floor,
our rising, one by one,
to play with loss, to practice,
what is *lived, to live*? What was that desire
to move through ourselves to the orange
cotton, agreed upon, passed
from one to another?

YASMIN

after the film Son of the Sheik

A woman in a sheer skirt, coins sewn to the hem, dances
in the background, the far background, behind
two men, rivals for her love. The sheik and the son of the sheik
face each other as Yasmin leaps and sways between them,
dragging her hem through the sand.
The grit, the jangle of her dance
are silent to the men.

One of the most famous scenes from the silent era:
At the sheik's foot an iron rod rests in the sand.
He picks it up, bends it
until the ends nearly meet.
Then he sets it in the sand, gently,
his palms skyward.
Now it is the son's turn to act.
His pale eyes shine like something polished by the sea.
He takes the rod, straightens it
as Yasmin dips, dragging her coins through the sand.

The sheik and the son of the sheik
are both Rudolph Valentino,
Rudolph split against himself by desire.

What is Yasmin's desire? Is it dancing she loves,
though she does this for money to support her cruel father?
Sometimes she sews the coins to her costume.
Sometimes she dances when no one is watching, like now,
the round mirrors on her headscarf throwing stars of light to the sun.
She dances to weave herself into the air.
She is not waiting for a man to claim her.
Her loneliness has nothing to do with love.

Yasmin's dance is made of circles, perfectly suited
to the small space allotted her.
It is anger Yasmin desires, behind Rudolph Valentino
and Rudolph Valentino, as she turns, thinking
All men are the same, making this passion serve her
movements, round and smooth and seamless.

THE DOCKS OF NEW YORK

after the film by Joseph von Sternberg, 1928

She wakes in an iron bed in a bare room
above a bar. She has slept through dancing and brawling,
the door being opened, a duffel bag dragged across the floor,
the near steps of the stevedore as he opened the bag, unfolded
the clothes he bought for her: a dress, a skirt
and a blouse with a ruffled collar.
Each of them will fit perfectly,
as if he had slept beside her, with his cheek
on her shoulder, so perfectly did he know her body
as he lifted her to shore.

She is sitting now, smoking a cigarette,
clothes draped from the headboard, the closet door
and the windowsill. She hugs her knees to her chest, pulls
                                        the sheet closer
and looks up as she did when she turned her face toward the moon
and she fell into the harbor,
let herself fall.

On the fresh waves moonlight blossomed like gardenias.
How could he not notice the whiteness in all the black?

He dives in. Easily, he finds her. Her arms are limp,
shining. If she opens her eyes now
she will push him away, he who bears her weight
without her consent. She will scream.
But she is sleeping the peace-filled sleep of those who want to die
as the water runs from her skirt
and from her hair, wetting the dock.
Already it is too late for him. He is in love with her.

She stubs out the cigarette and stands,
pulls the dress over her flesh-colored slip.
At this point, who doesn't know the story?
Who couldn't tell it in the time it takes
to fasten the buttons from nape to waist?
Yes, soon the stevedore will enter, shy
now that he is not touching her.
When he says his ship leaves tomorrow
she will touch her hair, and lean forward.

When they embrace they will look as they did
when they rose from the water,
the moon swimming toward them
though the waves would carry it to sea
if the waves had their way.

ADIRONDACK CURE, 1923

after Sheila M. Rothman

What recommended the cold, damp town
was that it was cold and damp.
No one would visit with cheap boxed candy,
with flowers in yellow water,
with—the worst—photographs
of the rest of the world on vacation,
smiling into sunlight as if there were no tomorrow.
We lived for tomorrow, in tomorrow.
No one who believed they were about to die
would go to the Adirondacks, to spend their last days
wrapped in blankets and fog,
no one in their right mind. So,
the sanitarium was a cheerful place,
full of jokes and lies.
You could happily spend hours
sitting on the deep porch, elbows propped
on the wide armrests of the low-slung chairs
named for these mountains.
They're not mountains, said the veterans of the cure
who'd sought health in New Mexico, in California.
A good-spirited argument ensued.
Some boasted of signing onto ships *to die*
by overwork, but to die healthy.
Under the overcast sky, timeless, there was time
to think, to breathe deeply
air cured with fir and pine, and snow
that stayed six months out of twelve, beautiful,
after all, in its pale blueness, echoing
that of the bed sheets and pillows.
The most serious cases sat on the porch
in their iron bedsteads, slept there all night.
In the morning, together, we looked across the porch railing

to the rope-marked walking path,
watched the strongest patients, pink-cheeked,
single-file, follow the doctor into the woods,
snowshoes slung over their shoulders.
It was possible to believe
the body can cure the body,
it surely can, given the right
amount of rest, right exercise, right air.
It hardly mattered to those of us who sat there,
wool mufflers wrapped up to our eyes,
it hardly mattered that death sat there among us,
that death's thigh was pressed against our own.
Death sat so close beside us
it had become part of our body.
Hadn't this always been the case?
I tell you, some of us fell in love.

WAKING IN THE MIDDLE OF THE NIGHT,
SHE REMEMBERS THEY FELL ASLEEP NAKED

Back to her,
face turned half into his pillow,
he has pulled his left knee toward his chest
as if he runs, long and steady,
through a wide field
with no thought of stopping.
He has run past the point of exhaustion,
now rides his body as if riding a horse,
having found what we call *second wind*—
air where there was none,
where there was capacity for none.
As in marriage there are times
when another day opens inside the day,
another night inside the night.

It is that time in early summer
for which there is no name:
the peonies heavy on their stems,
their decay rising sweet from the bushes.

One wakens while the other sleeps.
And then it will be his turn
to watch her lope over the grasses
toward a low fence, and clear it,
and circle back.

MADAME BEAUMONT

Madame Beaumont dyed her pale legs with a tea-colored stain.
Eyelids shiny blue, pale hair pinned at her temples,
she wore only black or beige, the colors of Paris during
                                                    the Occupation,
when each Friday the nun led Madame's class
to the Louvre, where some of the girls fell behind, hid,
brushing each other's hair in the wing of tombs.

We were in 10th grade, in 1969, in upstate New York,
memorizing, exploring tenses we might use in that strange land
the Future. Madame Beaumont asked us questions
and we fell silent, shy. We answered slowly.
If it was painful for Madame to hear the language of her childhood
battered by us, changed by us, she never said,
though there was one expression: sometimes, she would press
her index fingers together and touch her chin
as she listened.

I think now she was listening to memory,
as I think now that language is like a woman
standing in full sunlight. Her hair is tied at her nape
with a thin black ribbon. The wind swirls.
She is steady, but her hair is falling, slowly,
as if to say, *The sun shines here, and here. And here.*
I think the sun was shining outside the Louvre
so when the children went indoors
they were blind for a moment, and so fell silent.

Was Madame remembering braiding her friend's hair
or placing her hand on cool stone?
Was the memory painful to her, or good? *Good memory,*
we say, as if it were a dog that has carried in our slippers,
a newspaper, or run across a mine field
with a canister tied to his collar. During the War
dogs were trained for communication during battle.
They were trained to search rubble for survivors.

I see Madame sitting before us, crossing her leg
and tracing a circle with the toe of her shoe.
She is telling us that after the War her younger brother
carried out a secret he had kept for three years.
It was one of their mother's old handbags
and it was full of chocolate and, without a word, they ate.

THERE IS NO SUCH THING AS MOONLIGHT

after a photograph of Frida Kahlo and Diego Rivera

August 31, 1932 they stand on the roof
of the Detroit Institute of Arts, in full sunlight, each
holding a black card in front of their eyes
so they can stare at the solar eclipse.
He is six feet tall, and heavy.
A dark cord holds up his loose pants.
She stands to his shoulder, wears a shawl tucked at her waist.
Her skirt wraps three times around her hips.

He has begun to eat dinners with other women. Sometimes
he disappears for days. Honestly
he believes the tenderness he finds in himself
in these encounters is something he can bring
to his wife, as he brought her the turquoise earrings
that touch her shoulders as she tilts her head back.

She walks for hours through the Chinese neighborhood
buying silk for long skirts,
torn between wanting to hide and wanting to shimmer
as the light shimmers in this humid air
where they stand, sweating from the climb.

Together they wait for the moment of darkness,
the moon a black disk with its rim on fire,
the moon-sun like some ornament she would pin into her hair
for the pleasure he would find
in removing it

their arms growing heavy as they stand
here, imagining an eclipse, seeing in advance
the beauty they expect to see,
remembering how beauty feels in their bodies

which are light on one side
and dark on the other.

SEWING IN JANUARY

I.

Without trying to see, I saw:
the white-haired woman unrolling the bolt of fabric,
measuring it, thumb and forefinger
against a yardstick nailed to the edge of the counter.
The fabric is green. The pale sunlight
of December, 4 p.m., divides the room. A young woman waits.
Her fingertips rest on the edge of the counter
as if, playing a piano, she has hit the last chord
and waits for the vibrations to grow still inside of her.
All this seen as I walked quickly past,
for it is easier to see strangers than the ones I love.

Each year at this time, the days lengthening
like a hem let down as the child grows,
I remember the two women, the bolt of cloth
measured in arm lengths between them.
In January I always feel like sewing,
spreading fabric across my floor
and kneeling, pins held between my teeth.
I want to smooth the fabric
by running my hands across it in large circles,
want to pin tissue-paper to it for that moment the point disappears
and must be guided back, as my mother taught me.
I loved to go to the fabric shop with her.
I loved to play with the scraps, the tin of shirt buttons,
and I believe she loved it, too—
the powdery smell of new cotton,
the birdsong of pinking sheers as she trimmed the seams.
You must love the process, she taught me. *You should not hurry.*

Sometimes, before sleep, I rub my husband's back
and my hands look to me like my mother's hands
with their smooth skin, their rivery green veins.
Some day soon my body will be all I have of her.
I think of the two women in the shop, the apple-green bolt
growing thinner between them,
think of the sunlight in the shop
growing thinner until it became the dark.
I move my hands lightly across his back,
palms flat to feel the crests and hollows.
I listen to his breathing, slow, grow deeper,
moving my hands in circles
as if this movement could stop time, which is
made entirely of movement, as I have read
all the world's surfaces are made of movement, moving
so rapidly they seem to stand still.

This morning I lay on the examining table
as the doctor touched my breast.
As she moved her hands she looked at the bare wall,
where there was nothing: no window, no chart,
no pastel of boats on a lake.
My heartbeat was the sound of the fabric unfolding across the counter.
Inside my chest the two women stood, and the light
that came down to them from a high window,
leaving half the room in darkness.

All rooms are half darkness, says a friend of mine—
the life you lived there, and the life you wanted to live there.
I could see the orange tape measure, the black-handled scissors,
the small carbon paper the shopkeeper slips into the pad,
its texture like crepe-de-chine, like the skin of her hands,
as if we become what we touch,

as if we can be transformed by the smallest contact,
daily, or in passing.

II.
There is a blue glass bird on our windowsill.
Sometimes I lift the glass bird
for the pleasure of holding the cold weight of it,
the here-and-now of it,
my palm blue as if cupping water, as if to drink.
Daylight flies inside, in circles,
presses against the wings, folded and heavy,
a daylight that will not fade.
I can see it even tonight, in the dark,
even through the white curtain:
a small place
where starlight nests
casting enough light to read by,
enough to sew, if I sat very close.

I want to sew a shirt for my husband,
and a scarf wool on one side and silk on the other,
grey wool and yellow silk,
cut on the bias, like our days,
so it flows like water,
like the music the girl heard in the dim shop
as she watched the fabric cut, folded,
that day I saw her waiting
to take the green swath home
and turn it into something else.

WHAT IS THE LAKE?

She wades into the lake
in her white blouse and pink bermudas,
turns. She leans back and spreads her arms, lets
her feet rise. *It's beautiful,* she calls to me, meaning
the water and the sky, the lightness
of leaving shore.

She has decided to spend the rest of her life
at this lake. She will live in the dark green
cottage with rusted porch screens,
a telephone book dated 1942.
She is my age, 25, dark blond,
200 pounds. Her hands are like two white fish

as she swims an effortless backstroke.
Beneath, her long hair fans and swishes,
the motions of dream lifting sleep into song.
The last point where she can still touch bottom, she stops.
She stands, pulls the heavy rope of her hair
over one shoulder, twists it like a towel.

She shades her eyes with both hands.
She shades her eyes and looks at me, who
has tried to talk her back into town. I leave.
I drive away.

Twenty years later, some nights I dream of her,
this heavy woman who lived on the lake,
who floated on her back surrounded by clouds.
I swim toward her, but wake
before I touch her, tow her toward shore,
our arms salmon and orange in the evening sun.

If it is true, as I have read, that everything in a dream
represents the dreamer, then it is true
that the lake-woman, who is me, steps slowly into me,
leans her head back upon me, feels her/my feet rise
toward the round clouds that are also me.
But if this is not true, when I dream

of the heavy woman who loved the lake,
who dreamed herself part of the clouds,
when I dream of her, of whom do I dream,
of what do I dream that is not myself?
What is the lake? Who is the young woman on shore?

STUDY

for *Delores, Pam, Laura*

What if, at the decisive moment, I remember nothing I've read
as clearly as I remember that performer on The Ed Sullivan Show
with his ten poles and his ten white plates,
his bird-like dance that kept them afloat?
It's been thirty years and the image remains, behind it strains
of "Flight of the Bumblebee" played by the studio orchestra.
My mother is in the kitchen. I hear her rinsing plates.
My grandmother sits beside me with her stuffed-full purse:
nickels, church bulletins, half-sticks of gum.
There is the sound of her laugher, for I see
she is smiling in the TV's blue light.

What if Sidney's Astrophel and Stella are no more with me
than the names of the people I met at that party
the first time I was in college?
In the kitchen there was a footed bathtub
full of candles, white votives, burning.
It was meant to be beautiful, the hosts straining
for that, but not meant to be
as beautiful as it was—
it was of itself and not of them—
not meant to be as beautiful as it has become.
What if, at the decisive moment, the names
are lost to those blue shadow-flames whisking the porcelain,

the tips of firs dusting the sky
tonight? I read beside a window, waiting
for the sky to darken, for we have been told
tonight three stars will be visible at once
for the last time in this century.

I read in a house of four women, each of us reading
beside windows, feeling the cool breeze on the backs of our hands,
smelling the sour geraniums ignited by dew.

As if we can choose memory, I choose:
the four of us standing in the yard of our rented house.
We point at the sky, turn.
We turn and touch our eyes and turn, but as long as we turn
there is nothing to tell a person where, specifically, to look
under all the sky's
wobbling stars.

THOUGH THE GRASS

In the mid-nineteenth century there was a vogue
for lamb statues on children's gravestones,
maybe because the lamb symbolizes the Holy Child
or maybe because a lamb can drink from a baby bottle,
you can hold the bottle to its mouth and feel the pulling
all down your arm,
or maybe it's due simply to Victorian sentimentality,
which asks you to respond to an idea rather than experience
an emotion, the earliest lamb statues
carved from marble or granite. Later, there are plaster lambs
sprung from a mold, a seam running down the face
and along the spine, where the form overran the form.
All representation is reduction, I know this.
Late on a Saturday afternoon late in the next century
I have given myself a task so as to give form to my grief:
I must find all the gravestones marked with a lamb statue.
Looking at the lambs, some as small as shoeboxes,
some the size of a collie, I wonder if maybe
the lamb was never meant as a symbol
of anything other than itself: stone, plaster, a place
for shadows to slide and play.
I believe that everything needs to be a symbol of itself.
I have decided that I think so often of Gary's front porch
because, sitting there, I was fully myself.
I still think of the sagging wooden steps
where we sat in sunlight and in moonlight
and, once, as the rain became pouring rain,
the porch like every other porch on that street of company houses,
myself like any other woman who ever sat there
in a cap-sleeved housedress with her hair in a bun,
but fully myself. One night while Gary slept
I sat on the middle step, and this is as happy
as I have ever been, as I ever need to be.
The porch memory is my lamb statue. It shapes my grief
without containing it. It shapes me without containing me.

Recently, a friend of a friend, a man I hardly know,
looked steadily at me as I told him
I felt tired and sick—maybe the other way around,
I didn't know—
and he held the back of his hand to my forehead,
and then my cheeks.
Maybe the lamb statue on the child's grave
works like the acting method used in silent films,
where you hold the back of your hand to your forehead for *grief*.
The audience doesn't need to believe the actress
feels grief. That came later in the century.
It's enough she indicates to them the idea grief.
Allusion is not meaning. It is a gesture
toward meaning. What, possibly,
can one place on the grave of a child?
It occurs to me that maybe the lamb statuary,
cliché, vernacular, was a way of saying
no one is sole proprietor of his or her grief,
maybe saying this without believing, then, believing.
I want to know what carries us forward. Maybe it's form, the lamb,
that which will not change beneath the changing trees.
Of course grief changes, I know this. I've seen it.
What I mean is that loss is, somehow, carried forward
though the grass grows up around it.

REPLY

for Al Maginnes

No, I did not move to New York City
        to listen to jazz, and, truth
be told, I have not, to this day,
        gone to many clubs
but in January of 1980 or 81
        during a subway strike
the New York Public Library, where I worked,
        assigned those of us who lived in Queens
to jobs at local branches, mine
        beside a car dealership
at an intersection:
        Greek delis, a cheap pharmacy,
two fabric shops selling cottons and fake silks
        straight from the 1940s,
prints of polka-dots, and dice
        and flowers that do not exist in nature,
but should. Mostly, I remember lunch break,
        walking down 39th Avenue
that uncommonly warm winter, my coat open,
        my hands fisted in my pockets.
I skipped lunch to walk, bought a bagel
        I'd eat later, on the mandatory 15-minute break.
One of the fabric shops was owned by a woman
        who still styled her hair
in the short bangs and tight curls of the 50s,
        still zipped herself into a side-zippered dress,
the other shop run by a young black man
        in suit and narrow tie, fit
as a side-man, dapper, swell.
        When one ran a sale, so
did the other, women paused
        at the windows, *So,*
they're giving it away? all of it,
        those afternoons, like the musicians

who took their turn in the spotlight
          only to give it back, give it
back, the melody back again
          but larger, now, containing, now,
more silence, more give.
          The whole of 39th Avenue helped me
know what I took home
          each day, when I borrowed another record
from the library's donated collection,
          dusty maroon double-sets
with gold-lettering and dates,
          with black and white photographs
of some slowly self-destructing musician
          kept alive by music alone,
music and drink and smoke, a glamour
          I could never see
except for the clothes, the hats.
          Or maybe it was the music alone
that sustained them, music time itself,
          time enough for what had to be made
of it, of the small hours before light
          in a small light cast upon the stage
so the horn player could see, what?
          what did he need to see?
I listened to jazz all that winter
          and into spring, long after
the trains were running and I could travel
          under the river to work,
and under the river home
          and under the river to work,
head bobbing as the train swayed,
          humming.

THE HORSE LATITUDES

Navigators identified the Horse Latitudes by stars
and by noting how the waves were almost calm there,
                                          the nameless spot
where the ship moved slowly and more slowly, and everyone knew
the load would have to be lightened,
the horses chosen.

The smallest ones, which would bring the least the money, were led
to the rail, moonlight on their flanks, their teeth,
their watery eyes.
The smallest ones carried the moonlight down
to where they swam, following the ship
for some distance.

When a man and a woman make love
they can feel themselves pulled forward
by something not of their making,
call it what you will,
as they move through the dark, star-riddled water

but what of the man alone on deck?
He has chosen one star, and stares.
He pulls his coat closer. It is thin,
one of its buttons broken in half.
This is how he is dressed to start his new life

which must be different from the old:
serious, well-loved. What does he mean by these words?
They are ways to remember things he once saw—
two men stacking wood,
a woman and her child asleep in the same room—
in the way that the star will come to mean
something more than itself,

something he cannot anticipate now, standing at the rail,
the ship moving more and more swiftly,
hooves circling in its wake.

IVORY BRACELETS

I am fascinated by ivory bracelets, thick and heavy
and carved like cathedral doors, the pictures wrought from them

in layers, like successive rooms, this carving
reinforcing my belief that each surface hides a story

in bas-relief, an Atlantis where there is a table set for dinner
and a bracelet worn, at the moment her world ends,

by a girl holding a cup with two hands.

I stare into store windows at these bracelets on blue velvet
but see only a Braille in the polished, buttery ivory

which is the color of my grandfather's fingernails
thickened and hardened by 43 years in the shoe factory.

The carvings could be the long room I saw once
when I was five years old, the workbenches high as my forehead.

It was piecework. I didn't know what I saw
but I saw the leather tongues strung together in stacks,

each stack with a paper tag to be saved, counted at
                                          the end of the week,
dangling, waving in the breeze from the fans.

I saw the brooms, the canvas bins for scraps,
beneath the benches, pots: you wouldn't leave your work to pee.

Someone opened the window, which looked like a barn door
and slid sideways, and this I remember best: how blue the sky looked
over the factories' tar roofs.

On certain days the sky is the color of ivory
but ivory is a more substantive beauty, throughout time

associated with power and death.
When it circles the wrist

it is often worn in pairs that clack dully together
or worn singly, as those things we prize most.

When I look at an ivory bracelet I want to imagine
that it is carved with figures of both animals and humans

and the men carry bowls to the horses,
who lower their heads and drink

and the women, tall, are naked and shaded by fir trees,
beyond the trees a stream.

I know this is too much for one bracelet
but that is how it is true to life. The pieces

of this story cannot be woven together.
I want to imagine the stories on the bracelet

cover time, and cross it, in harmony
and some of the Braille is in fact for the blind

and some of the shadow opaque,
the ivory dark-veined, flawed.

I am fascinated by what has been left out
to create the beautiful shapes, and deepen them.

I want to imagine that nothing died for this.

THRIFT SHOP

The round collars and pearlized buttons,
the yellow dacron blouses embroidered
with tic-tac-toe's, with Eiffel Towers,
the pink cotton skirts printed with cats,
with bow ties, with haystacks, maybe
this is like standing in the breeze
with my mother, holding the clothespins for her
as she raised the sheets, spread them
into unbelievable size.
I remember I put my hand on her sanded foot.
Her nail polish was Honeybee Pink
like the angora sweater sagging on its hanger,
like the border on the silk kerchief
sporting scenes from Shakespeare.
And there are the aprons the Slovak women
wore over their dresses in the shoe factory,
calico, the flowers too small to name.
There is the plaid housecoat of the neighbor
who gave me orange juice in a big glass,
she who covered her back lawn
with rocks she'd found in the river
then painted chalky blue, the color
of the quilted robe, of the plastic bracelet
in the "$1" box beside the cash register.
What is it that makes me force this bracelet
over my knuckles? What do I want?
There is a mint green that contains starlight,
there is the pink of the cream after strawberries-
and-cream, permutations of light flowing back
through itself, held, honored.
But there is also linen, unbleached,
and even its mendings I love, the loose crosshatch
of repair, of faith in repair.
When my grandmother's sisters laid her coats
across her bed, and opened her jewelry box,

I didn't want the rhinestone earrings
she'd once let me try on, telling me that one day
I'd be able to wear those tight clips
without feeling them hurt me.
I touch a housedress with house-shaped buttons,
party aprons printed with crescents of melon,
with playing cards, with fans.
When my grandmother got cancer I could see
at her throat the skin turned to charcoal
and I didn't touch her anymore.
In a hatbox I find gloves smooth as petals,
on a shelf, clutch bags and veiled hats.
There are silk flowers that can be pinned
onto the hats, magenta, orange, blue.
I don't remember touching my grandmother ever again.

BIRD FIGURINES

There is one on nearly every shelf of the antique shop,
and on walls, on tables, under tables:
the tin, the china, the paper mache
bluebirds and jays and chickadees,
the eagles carved out of cherry or walnut.
It is as if, in a century of work and sickness,
the light dim, the food scant and quickly cooling,
in the few idle minutes before sleep
people said, "Now it is time
to work on my bird figurine."
The woman settles her child to bed, and resumes
stuffing straw into a house wren pin cushion,
or, she paints a robin onto a teacup, partner to the saucer
brightened with a nest, three moonlit eggs.
The man still wearing the sweat of the field
leans toward the fire, carries a piece of it
to the top of a blanket chest, wherein he burns
a mallard, an unfortunate horse-like eye.
And this is not to mention the marble penguins
flanking the pen holder,
the red geese circling the cereal bowl,
the wall sconce shaped like the head of a parrot,
and not to mention the needlework,
the bridal veil, its scalloped edge filmy with swans,
the baby sweater with its duck-shaped pockets.
From the hat rack topped with an owl
to the foot stool upholstered with needlework peacocks,
it becomes possible to imagine a bird figure on every surface,
and to imagine the hands perched above fabric,
stitching silk threads into tail feathers and talons,
to imagine the fingers dipping into water
and swooping across clay, finding
that place where the throat swells into breast,
that place where we forget we cannot fly
except into our work.

GIRLS' SCHOOL

for Joanne Devereaux

In the rectangular photograph three feet wide
the graduating class of Vassar, 1923,
sits four-deep on the wide lawn,
their flat collars and bowed neckerchiefs
making them look ten years younger
than they are.
Perhaps the photographer has said something truly funny
in order to make the 98 women smile so naturally
but more likely the photographer is silent, preoccupied
with the mechanics of process
while the women talk among themselves, happy.
They are happy to be sitting in the sun bare-headed,
collars open, hands poised as scholars' hands: idle,
half-closed upon themselves like the hands of sleepers
cupping water to the mouth of dreams.
The photo is sepia, faded almost to butter
at the edges, so those women at the ends of the rows
look ghost-like. Their eyes and round chins
seem printed on air, seem like field flowers
embedded in amber.
There are wild violets on this lawn,
their citrine stems lost among the dark green.
The grass is slightly damp, though the women
do not notice this until they stand,
their skirts clinging, their white stockings
stained yellow-green at the ankle.
But this is the moment before standing,
or the moment before that,
98 women with their lives spread out before them
as this class is spread before a pale brick building.
Some have already moved forward from this place.
You can see this in the tilt of a head,
the twist of a waist, the arm resting lightly

on the arm of another.
Some of the women of this graduating class of '23
have cut their hair,
and some still wear their hair long, pinned softly up.
Some have tucked violets into their hair.
Some have tucked violets into each other's hair.

TAG SALE

Someone could part with it,
the 2" by 3" gold metal frame
containing

the ocean, far from land,
up close, so it looks
like the Pyrenees, or an X-ray

or parachute silk
spread upon damp grass
as the jumper slips free

but it is the ocean,
above sepia letters
wavering in the lower margin,

Flying Fish.
Someone leaned over the edge
of the boat, snapped

what only her eye,
or mind's eye,
caught: a sliver

of silver among silver,
swift crescent
lifting sunlight

toward sun,
threading salt air to wave
as it curves

down, to the scintillant erasure
of sun-on-water
on which the boat traveled,

followed.
What was left for her
after the fish

disappeared?
Water, waters,

embracing light, turning light,
the ocean like the mind
turning a thought

over, finding
in that thought
something that rises

into light,
maybe light itself

a movement
that makes one want
to say something

likewise brilliant,
about looking, or longing,
or loss

to lean,
to lean from the boat

to lean from the boat
out over the waters.

FRIDAY MEDITATION

Every Friday a man I have never seen enters my building and shouts
at the woman who used to be his wife, his voice angry at the world
he carries, angry at the curse words that will not carry his anger,
which fall short of what he needs them to be
and so grow louder, as their son
hums one note over and over so he will not hear
what I hear these two floors above
through the walls that conduct our lives better than we do.
I do nothing to help. I grow angry at the man
for destroying my silence.

Every Friday the woman and boy wait. I have forgotten him.
I am in the process of forgetting everything I have ever known
sitting on the floor, my eyes closed,
my anger leaving, my sadness, everything
emptying so I will be able to fill myself again
with the simplest of things:
the sound of heat in the radiators,
the smell of wool.
I have forgotten the man. And then I remember.

Cruel how things once strange, unthinkable, become familiar
or, for that matter, how anything becomes familiar.
When I first heard there are people who buy new furniture
and whip it with chains, gash it, to make it valuable
I thought this foolish until one day it wasn't.
One day it became just another lunge toward beauty, another way
to live, and now it reminds me of how the man's voice
snaps the air, wraps around whatever it touches,
for surely this shouting is what the boy sleeps on every night,
this is the table at which he eats,
and when the man leaves the apartment with their son
this is what the woman leans on and sinks down into.

THE TRAIN PASSES THROUGH

The train passes through Harlem
      like a low-flying plane,

close enough that I can begin
      to read the words brush-painted,

meticulously, on the boarded-over windows
      of the brick apartment house on Broadway and 123rd,

a six-story building that tells one story
      in foot-high letters of flat black paint,

some words in cherry red, like when Jesus speaks
      in the Bible.

Twenty-four white fireman and one
      black fireman responded

says the first window of eighteen—
      as far as I can read before

it is gone, behind me, words hanging in the air
      as did the man, I imagine, who wrote them.

Think of it: a man suspended by a rope at his waist
      stands on the side of a fire-gutted building, writing.

From a distance, he looks like a letter himself,
      a capital T, an H.

He is a black man, and this
      is where he is safest, high above the street.

I wonder if anyone watched him work,
      if his words called people together,

to the foot of the building,
        to its majestic shadow.

I wonder if anyone riding this train ever stood, ran
        to the back of the train, car by car,

to read the man's words, straight to the end
        of the story, the final word

in red: *Now.* Exclamation point.
        As I wonder, the train is already

in another world, *now*
        a beige meadowland dotted with lumber

yards, and truck yards.
        There are small houses,

low to the ground, each with a small yard
        surrounded by chain-link fence.

And there are storehouses, cement blocks
        painted pale blue,

for all that does not fit
        into the small houses:

tables, chairs, single-beds,
        maybe a bicycle,

items that exist for the owners
        as ideas only, abstractions, as in

what Plato would have us call *the ideal world,*
        which is not the world we know.

It is not, by definition, a world we can know.
     I have read this, time and again,

in what passes by the train window.
     Miles ahead, I wonder what the burned-out building

says to the sky,
     what the sky says back.

What is supposed to happen *Now?*

ON HIS DEATHBED THE ACROBAT
TELLS HIS DAUGHTER TO BUY LAND

I see now
it was never the sky
I wanted

though for years I perfected
leaps and dives, arching, curling
tucking my chin hard into my chest
to spin free
far above my shadow.

Now I see
it was always the earth
its mysterious pull
I was celebrating.
It was always to return
to the earth's hard bargain, on two feet
my arms spread like wings.

There are enough birds, Edith.
The air is full of seeds
far better than we can ever be—
invisible, merciful.
When I watched you pass the hat
I wanted to crawl into our wagon
and lie with my hands crossed over my chest.
I wanted to count the potatoes and flour
and find for once enough.
I wanted to melt my father's gold watch
and buy you a horse
and shoes of thin leather.

Remember I never asked you
to walk on your hands.
I respected your fear of heights,
of the fireworks we set off
at the end of the show.

The hard-packed earth at the center of town
where the people gathered,
their thin shoulders touching,
that was my passion.

Remember before each trick
it was the red earth
I rubbed into my palms.

LABYRINTHITIS

I say the room is spinning
though it is only one part of the room
that spins, repeatedly, past.
Six days in August I lie in bed and note and note
the inaccuracy of this expression.
Labyrinthitis, I am told. It is the heat. It is the air full of seed.
It is my own need to lie in bed for six days, spinning.
The room is not spinning. The window
is sliding, smoothly, left to right,
simultaneously reappearing
where it began, sliding.
Repetition is the seed of beauty, says Kundera, says Chesterton,
says Olatunji, Nigerian drummer in carnation-pink robes.
This window is not beautiful except by personification,
its human-like need to trace and retrace. Six days in August
I do not dress, lie naked and silent, alone.
The window slides across the wall like a thrown egg.
I say the room is spinning because I believe I am the center.
I say the room is spinning because I have made
a house of illusion, and lived inside of it.
I slept in the room with the picture of the desert on the wall,
the dark-eyed man who taught me the extremes of that climate.
In spring we drove to auctions, furnishing the house,
woke to the sound of metal hitting rock, our neighbor
tilling earth, tying white string from stake to stake.
I say the room is spinning because one part of the room
stands for the whole, as I would say my entire life
is told in what I remember: my grandmother crouching
in the tomato garden, the green-topped tomatoes,
the pale green eyes of my lover watching my hands
as I tell him of that garden, of carrying the cool tomatoes
in a straw basket, into the house. As I tell him
I am lifting the basket. It swings on my arm.

I say the room is spinning because I live with inaccuracy,
with approximation, with the moment
the red fruit on its frail stem
is lifted, and let hung.
I say the room is spinning, finally,
because that is how we speak of it.
That is how we understand,
approximately, in passing.

THIS

for David

Midway through "Parlor, Bedroom, Bath," where Buster Keaton
signs the hotel guest registry
while rainwater pours from his golf bag
erasing the name he keeps writing, water flowing
across the counter and down his pant leg to the marble floor,
I heard my laugh as it must sound to you, David—
a bit surprised, lovely. Keaton caps the pen
and when he turns, it's no surprise really,
he falls flat, and he rises
and falls again. He pulls himself up by his suitcase
and then he falls over his suitcase.
At this point I miss you terribly.
I want to call you and say Yes.
Then the others come to Keaton's aid:
the porter, the bystander, the recently-jilted
woman Keaton is pretending to seduce
for the sake of her lover's jealousy.
For a full five minutes all four of them,
in all combinations, slip and splat out flat
on the lobby floor, with no thought of leaving
that treacherous spot,
no thought of crawling off to safety.
It's one of those scenes where goofiness deepens
into deep goofiness, and something beyond.
No one speaks, or tries to speak.
The only sound is the squeak of shoe soles.
When they hold each other I think they are like one body, almost,
but then I decide they are like twenty bodies, or a hundred,
approximating one.
As I watch I think all of them, all one hundred of them,
have fallen under a spell where they believe
they cannot be hurt, and so they cannot.

They skate, on all parts of their bodies,
across the floor so shiny it's become invisible
and they, too, in sympathy, have become invisible
in the crowded lobby where no one notices
this awkward, charmed dance.
David, I want to risk
breaking an arm or a leg of this poem
by saying that after the movie the scene played on
in my head until I was amazed.
How is it the dance with gravity frees them?
I was amazed by my desire to have you beside me, watching
this scene where the feet, all two hundred of them, shuffle
up, into the air.

LISTENING TO THE POEM

for P. Schultz and National Public Radio

I.
What choice do I have but to stand and begin sweeping the
                                        kitchen floor
as I listen to songs of the guardian angel who assaults you with care,
of the diligent light, of our city's faithful poor?
I am torn between my desire to dance and to be of use.
I stroke straw across linoleum and hear the sea
because of the possibilities of song, the stray bits of breadcrumb,
of soot swept off the windowsill, up from the thruway,
the gathering of these as my mother gathered them
nightly, just before sleep, the rest of us already in dream
as she swept the floor and set the table for breakfast.

II.
Sweeping, I am separate from the broom. I won't say otherwise.
But my palms are the headlights of a car driving home through
                                        the rain
and my shoulders are the grooved cups where the mollusk lived
and my legs, they are strong. Beneath my ribs I carry
my ration of darkness, black as earth that sticks to the wagon's wheel.
My face is bowed, as with prayer.

What must be done and what can be left undone?
The sun is setting as your voice winds the poem
down, as if placing a round object on a table
and steadying it. Outside, my neighbor kneels in the dirt, planting
starlight between the tomatoes, bending, digging, lifting
                                        the fecund dark
into the dark that bears nothing, not even grief.

I listen to a poem as I sweep my kitchen floor, and when I finish
I will wash the green bowl left in the sink
and I will dry it, because that is what I was taught.
Before sleep we must put our houses in order.

III.
What joins one day to the next is dark and damp
and we have named it night. We trust our dreams to it, though
we will not admit this. Sometimes we wake in the middle of it,
needing water. We have dreamt of the ocean, our arms young and tan.
We saw the short hairs at our lover's temples, bleached white as bone,
and we wake knowing it is not the night that frightens us.
It is our certainty that our limits define us.
It is our certainty, in the face of our uncertainty
that love does not end, that love's limits define it.
It is our calm certainty that the first breath of silence
after Ben Webster's "Chelsea Bridge" is another beat,
somehow inside our chest, and connected
to whatever we could possibly say.

AUGUST EVENING

August evening, low clouds stream
orange and pink like the silk scarves
dyed for the stores uptown by the tenement worker
photographed circa 1920: strings strung across her

kitchen, she walks with one hand before her
like a blind woman among the brilliant scarves—
the photo hand-tinted—scarves gold, vermilion, chartreuse.
On evenings like this my grandmother's three sisters

carried their kitchen table out to the garden.
They stood in their open-toed terry slippers
in the damp grass, putting their arms through the arms
of the flowered aprons, each tying the bow

        at the small of her back,
her shadow like cricket or dragonfly
on the gold-green lawn.
All day, work in the shoe factory

and, now, work of her own choosing,
piles of peas pried from their sleep,
plucked and sorted, fingertips tapping on the tin-topped table.
Only one of the sisters stood in the garden

at one time, as if any more would be too much joy,
but I was allowed to follow,
placing my feet into her footprints
in the fragrant dirt. She lifted a cool tomato,

asked me if she should pick it
or leave it until tomorrow.
I carried the blue mixing bowl of snap-peas
until it got too heavy.

Soon, my grandmother would carry the bowl into the house
and I would climb onto a step-ladder beside the sink.
I would swoosh water inside of the empty bowl.
My grandmother would help me lift it to the counter,

turn it upside-down on a towel.
Soon, not yet. The sun had set
but the clouds stirred enough light to work by,
pink light, along our arms and hair,

along the white lip of the bowl
we called our life,
oh, without naming it *life*,
without calling it work.

TV COOKING SHOWS

Whether it is the one with the short woman
who begins each segment by unscrolling a map of Italy
and touching it with a wooden spoon
or the one with the Spanish man who runs onto the set
blowing kisses,
there is a glass bowl
of julienne carrots and fresh sprouts,
and the tossing of them, lightly.
There is the wire whisk folding air
into butter, butter into air,
the professional-quality spatula getting the last of it,
whatever it is,
from the sides of the bowl.
Where else can you see such joy—
the eggplant lifted shoulder-high,
slowly turned under the lights,
the green pepper chopped into perfect cubes,
shining, a mosaic in a holy place.
Sometimes I live behind a glass wall.
I can see the world but not hear it.
I want nothing of it.
These cooks will touch anything with their hands.
They enjoy it. They do not worry about stains or clean-up.
Seasoning sprinkles like magic from their thumbs.
They toss shallots into olive oil with a little butter
(it's been heating, unnoticed, on a side burner)
and a microphone picks up the sizzle,
which is not the sound of rain falling on a lake.
It is not the sound of a brush, pulling,
static, through long hair.
It is the sound, exactly, of itself.
Then the cook turns to another item on the menu,
the baked apple or the brandy-stewed pear,
turning, occasionally, back to the shallots,
this meal a dance with the entire kitchen.
I love the show where three chefs compete

to create the best meal, which must include three ingredients
strange or ordinary—banana peel, kumquat, potato.
Nothing goes to waste on the cooking shows, nothing.
Sometimes, in the glass wall, I see my own reflection.
I look like my mother or my youngest sister,
my mother or my youngest sister looking at me,
which is to say I look at myself looking at myself.
There are mirrors on the ceiling of the studio kitchen
so you can see the cook's hands and look directly
into the bowls and pans and skillets, see from above
the knife, the knife repeatedly chopping on the wooden board
ingredients that could have been chopped in a food processor.
In these kitchens anything is possible.
After you peel from the counter your fresh-made pasta
and wrap it barber-pole style around a wooden skewer
and let it dry for six or seven minutes
you can coax it free, slip it into boiling salted water
and it will retain its spiral shape, your beautiful fusilli.
Who can believe it would keep its shape?
The desserts, too, astound, say, the lemon crepe
with its play of sweet and sour,
but what is sweeter
than the studio audience at the cooking show?
From nine years to eighty, they crane, they part their lips,
they lift their shoulders in anticipation, in pleasure—
Fennel? Can it be she will add fennel?
Later, oh, later they will try this at home, this
irreproducible dish they will work on and riff on
for the rest of the season.
This is ontology, not epistemology. This is metaphysics.
Members of the audience look as though they are in heaven:
unselfconscious, satisfied even before they eat.
They will, many of them, eat
while the camera studies their faces.
Before speaking, they will take their time to taste,
lips wet, sometimes chins wet
as they face the camera without seeing the camera.
Presentation counts, everyone knows this.

The food must be served with flourish,
the last of the sauce dribbled over the entire plate, so
as to unify and, simultaneously, play up
the various textures.
But this presentation is not for the camera,
as none of this is, not really. It is food.
And we are supposed to eat it.
And be glad to grow hungry again.

GERTRUDE STEIN SINGING

The caption says that Gertrude Stein
is "singing her favorite song"
while sitting on a stone wall
at the top of a hill. Behind her
there is only sky, the sky of Italy
or the sky of southern France, or,
if you consider the earth's turning,
both Italy and southern France,
perhaps the very sky under which I sit
today, minus the song, a North American sky
of late August, which has turned the grasses brown
from heat or age, their season gone.
If I were to take off my shoes
and walk through the parched grass
my feet would prickle as my father says
your entire body prickles after a stroke,
ever after. "Always?" I ask him.
His answer: "More or less."

What song can be sung
when *more* and *less* are the same,
what balance be struck?
The stone walls in my part of the world
are low and rounded, mark boundaries
of farms long gone wild: apple, dairy,
land where stones swam like schools of fish beneath the snow,
come spring the first harvest a harvest of shale and mica,
a land too harsh for grapes, where wine meant
Communion, and not with nature.
You could always step over these walls without strain
for they were more the idea *wall* than wall,
which is more wall than stone. Who sang?
I want to know, who sang? As I drive I stare

at the woods and the fields and think of my family,
who never traveled, who crossed the ocean once,
to get here, and called it enough.
Stein, near 60, sings as the stone wall takes her
its long arc round the world.
She feels the long arc of the world in her song.
What song? I want to know, what song does she sing,
and why?

CROWS FLY OVER

after Wil Barnett after Emily Dickinson

Back to us
long skirted
hands folded

she is a keyhole
against the sky

presumably
watching the crows
fly toward the low hill

away,
for why
would she walk

so far
to close her eyes?

In her dark clothes,
her long dark hair
wound, pinned

she is a kind of night
in this noon light.

It is possible
her narrow body blocks
something only she can see—

a horse, perhaps,
like an ivory charm
on the horizon.

If she reached out
it would walk
the hills of her palm

this horse perhaps
she must lead home

this horse perhaps
she imagines,
its eyes and mouth

dark as the crows,
iridescent
and gone.

COUNTRY

Country can mean this place, far from a city,
far from towns, a nameless place
of two-lane highways—202, 306, 81—
called *routes*, tangled with pines
and hemlocks and pink hydrangeas bloomed, improbably,
a third time this year, a place of stone walls,
of long driveways where children stand at 7 a.m.
waiting for the school bus, to travel roads named
for families long gone, who built the frame houses
that smell, now, of soil, and sink into the soil.
The children wait beneath trees that have not waited
for the October air to frost, but have rushed ahead
into autumn, bottle-green given way to claret and honey
and brown. I drive this road to work and imagine
I know the three brothers who live in the yellow house
barely visible from the road, house the color of dust on glass.
Their skin is so pale it is blue at the temples.
Maybe one day the eldest will repair the car
parked beside the porch, repair it and smash it into a tree,
and maybe one will drive off in a stranger's car,
a kind stranger who has stopped for the hitch hiker
in whom he sees one of his lost selves. The other?
Maybe he will raise a family, live in this house.
Or maybe not: one become a doctor, the other two
start a business, sell this land to a developer.
Because I drive past, their world is silent,
like that of the boy named William
who went through elementary school with me.
He followed his twin, Barbara, everywhere,
sat with his desk pressed up against hers,
for years not speaking except to her.
Thirty-five years ago, that is the way it was:
you wore a *flesh*-colored hearing aid
with a wire that ran into your collar
and you wore a look of panic sealed in your eyes,

your thick tongue. I do not like to remember him
as I do not like to think, after I've gotten to work,
about the children standing in the driveway
beside the magnificent, unkempt hydrangeas
with their cheap blue knapsacks, soiled, already tearing.
These children are not mine. I do not like to think of their house,
filmy, like one of those prints of *nature*
manufactured in Manhattan on West 24th Street in the 1920s:
a pond, a rim of trees, maybe a horse in the foreground,
an idealized *country* to hang in the dining room
or at the top of the stairs. You see them in antique shops,
lush prints with velvety greens, in chestnut frames,
behind heavy glass. I have seen the school bus two or three times.
It is the short kind, sent out for crippled kids, or the aged,
and there is always someone inside
standing, trying to coax a window up or down,
the driver glaring at the child in the rear-view mirror.
The beautiful leaves' reflections
float across the child's face, as if he has drowned in the pond.
It's not that I really care about the child but, still,
I don't want to think about him or her, not when
I've gotten to work early, not when I'm trying
to name the trees' colors: mahogany, claret, honey,
Moroccan leather, red.

AT THE BEACH

after Edouard Manet

How does the artist first see
it is worth painting,
this long-married couple

who have arranged themselves
on the sand? The woman is heavy,
wears yards of grey silk,

hat sheathed with a veil,
the man in black suit coat
tight at the armpits,

his sleeve crusted with salt.
What is it about these two
that is promising

to the painter,
who has a broad palette
but needs only the black and the white,

a touch of raw umber,
to tell everything
that needs to be told?

He sketches without being noticed
on a notepad no bigger than his palm
(he could be marking a train schedule,

adjusting a cuff-link)
while the couple sits on their tiny white blanket
and stares at the sea,

stares at the sea
whose waves will be represented
by white paper, untouched

where the light touched them,
causing the woman to shade her eyes
and look down.

It is late summer but surely
there is a green park
where young lovers picnic,

the blue shade of a poplar
drifting slowly over a white plate
of half-eaten pear, a rose-crusted bread.

The painter walked past the park,
walked until he was tired,
and sat. *Whatever I see,*

he said to himself.
Whatever I see
from here.